Bible For Girls: Great Bible Stories For Girls

Speedy Publishing LLC
40 E. Main St. #1156
Newark, DE 19711

www.speedypublishing.com

9781681275758
First Printed January 13, 2015

God's Green Thumb

Back in the day when God first made the Earth, God looked down and he saw that there was no one to take care of it.

So God reached down into the ground and scooped up some stuff from the earth. He took the stuff from the earth into his hands and formed it into a man. But the man just laid there on the ground like a lump of clay. There was no life in him. So God bent down again and breathed into the man - and the man became alive!

The man's body was made from the earth, but his life came from the breath of God. Always remember that. Your life is the breath of God.

God called the man, 'Adam.'

Then God planted a garden in Eden for Adam to live in. And since God is God, he is a pretty good gardener. He planted all kinds of trees in his garden; apple trees, and pear trees, banana trees and mango trees, fig trees and who knows what other kinds of trees in his garden. God wanted to make sure there was plenty of good things to eat.

In the middle of the garden God also planted two special trees. One was called the Tree of Life, and the other was called the Tree of the Knowledge of Good and Evil.

And God made a stream of clear, cool water to flow through the middle of the garden to water it and keep it green.

Then God brought Adam to the garden and he told him, "Take care of my garden. You may eat the fruit of any of the trees that I have made to grow there. But be careful. Do not eat any of the fruit from the tree of the Knowledge of Good and Evil. If you eat any of that fruit, you will die."

So Adam began to live and work in the garden God had made for him.

The garden was a wonderful, beautiful place.

But Adam was lonely.

Even though the garden God had made for him was the most beautiful place there could ever be, Adam was lonely.

Adam needed some company. So God reached into the ground again and took some more stuff from the earth. This time he made every kind of animal and every kind of bird. He brought them all to Adam to see what he would call them.

It must have taken a long, long time to think up all those names!

But even with all the animals around to keep him company, God saw that Adam was still sad. Monkeys are fun to play with, but they don't have very much to say.

So God made Adam fall asleep, and while Adam was sleeping, God took one of his ribs.

God took Adam's rib and he made a woman from it. When Adam woke up, God brought Eve to him, and Adam said,

“At last! Here is someone like me! Her bones were made from my bones, and her body was made from my body. I will call her ‘woman’ because that means she was taken out of man.”

At last Adam was happy.

And so Adam and Eve lived together in God’s garden. And do you know what? They were naked and nobody cared.

Things were going along quite nicely in the perfect place that God had made for Adam and Eve. But then one perfect, warm sunny day, Eve was walking through the garden. And there, in the middle of the garden, she met the serpent.

You need to know that the serpent was the one we call the devil, or sometimes we call him Satan. Satan is an angel who decided he didn't want to do what God said anymore, so God sent him out of heaven. And from that day on, Satan became God's enemy.

So the serpent said to Eve,

"Did God really tell you that you couldn't eat the fruit from any tree in the garden?"

That's not what God said at all, and Eve knew it. So she said to the serpent,

"God said we may eat the fruit from any tree in the garden - except the fruit from the tree of the Knowledge of Good and Evil. If we even touch that fruit, we will die." Well, that wasn't quite true either, was it. God never said anything about touching the fruit.

The serpent answered, "That's not true at all! You will not die! God only said that because he knows if you eat that fruit you will become like him. You will become wise. You will know the difference between right and wrong."

And this is where Eve made her big mistake.

Instead of leaving right then, she stayed a while. She saw that the fruit on the tree looked very good. And she started thinking how nice it would be to be like God and know everything. But she also knew that God had said not to eat the fruit from that tree. Except now she was starting to think maybe it would be okay anyway. That fruit did look good. And the more she looked at it, the more she wanted it - and the more she forgot what God had said.

So Eve took some of the fruit, and she ate it.

And she gave some to Adam, and he ate it.

And all of a sudden they knew that they were naked.

Before that they were like little kids who run around naked and nobody cares - because little kids don't know any better. That's how Adam and Eve were before they ate the fruit God told them not to. Before that, they didn't know any better. They didn't know the difference between right and wrong. Now they did. Now they knew they were naked. And they were embarrassed.

Later that day...

God was walking through the garden in the cool of the evening as he liked to do. But when Adam and Eve heard him coming they hid from him in the bushes. They were embarrassed and afraid. God called to them, "Adam! Eve! Where are you?"

Adam answered from behind the bushes, "Right here, Lord... I heard you coming... so I hid from you... because I am naked."

"Who told you that you were naked?" God asked. "Did you eat the fruit I told not to eat?" God knew that he had. He always knows.

"It wasn't me!" Adam said, "the woman you gave me, she made me do it!"

So God said to Eve, "Is that true?"

And Eve said, "It wasn't me! The serpent made me do it!"

They were in big trouble now.

They knew God said not to eat the fruit from the tree of the Knowledge of Good and Evil. But they did it anyway. They turned away from the way God wanted them to go. They turned away from God.

Adam and Eve brought sin into God's perfect world.

Even though Adam tried to blame Eve for eating the fruit, and Eve tried to blame the serpent, God knew the truth. They all had disobeyed him.

So first, God said to the serpent,

"Because you lied to my children and tricked them into disobeying me, you will crawl on your belly from this day on, and you will eat dust as long as you live."

And then, because God knows what is going to happen today and every day after that, he said to the serpent (remember, the serpent was really Satan), "You will hate Eve and her children, and all the people who are ever born after them. You will be their enemy. And you will do everything you can to hurt them. You will do everything you can to keep them from knowing how much I love them. But one day a child will be born. You will bite his heel, but he will crush your head."

Now God turned to Adam and Eve.

God said to Eve, "Because you sinned and disobeyed me, this is what is going to happen. When you have children, it will not be easy. It is going to hurt. "

And he said to Adam, "Because you disobeyed me, you will have to work hard all your life for the food you eat and the things you need. Weeds and prickly things will grow along with your food, and you will sweat to make things grow. All your life you will have trouble."

And he said to both of them, "And then one day you will die, just as I said you would. I made your bodies from the dust from the ground, and one day they will become dust in the ground again."

All this happened because Adam and Eve disobeyed God.

So God made clothes out of animal skins for Adam and Eve to wear. And then God sent them out of the beautiful, perfect garden he had made for them. God put an angel with a flaming sword on guard at the graden's gate to protect the perfect place from the terrible things sin can do.

Adam and Eve began to learn that when we choose to do what we want instead of what God wants, we ruin the good things God has made for us.

But even though Adam and Eve had sinned, God still loved them.

The very moment Adam and Eve disobeyed God, sin came between God and his children.

Because we are all God's children, sin has separated us all from God. We can't live apart from God, so now God had to make a way to bring us back to him. And that is what the rest of the Bible is all about!

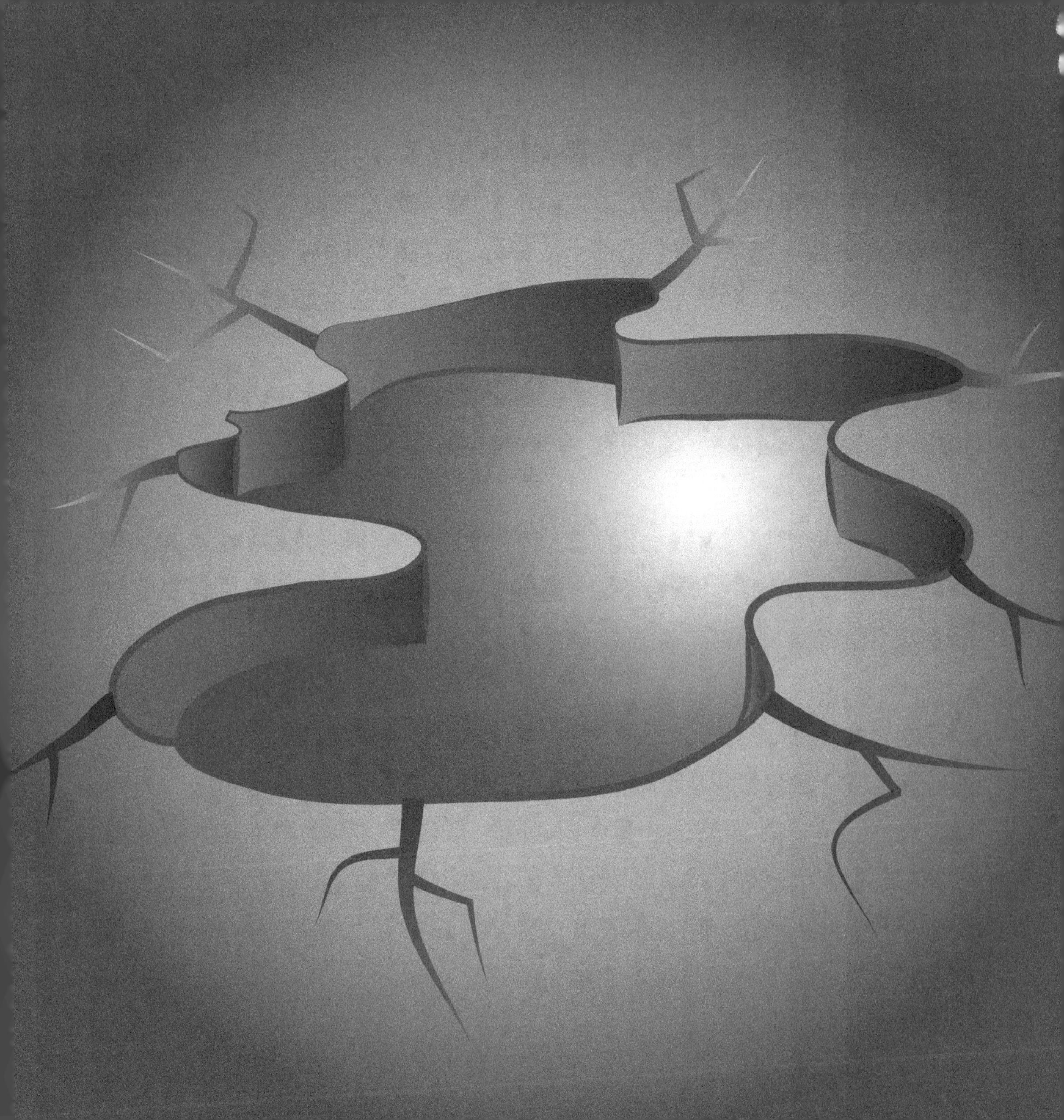

The Pits

"Joseph!"

"Here I am!" Joseph answered his father one day.

"Go see what your brothers are up to."

"Yes, Father," Joseph said.

Joseph's 10 older brothers were out in the pastures tending their sheep, and Jacob wanted to know how they were. And so he sent Joseph out to check on them. Little brothers are good at spying for their parents! And there's ANOTHER reason why sometimes they aren't liked very well by their older brothers and sisters!

But it wasn't really that Jacob was spying on his sons. He cared about all his children deeply, and he wanted to make sure they were all right. He also knew that people can get into trouble when they think that no one is watching.

And he was right.

So Joseph set out for the distant pastures.

But he couldn't find his brothers anywhere. Once again, they weren't where they said they would be.

A stranger found Joseph wandering around in the fields.

"Are you looking for something?" the stranger asked.

"I am looking for my brothers - the sons of Israel. Do you know where they are?"

"Sure do," the stranger said. "They were here a while ago. I heard them say that they were going to go to Dothan."

"Thanks!" Joseph said, and he began to walk to Dothan.

He was still a ways away, when the colors of his coat, shining in the bright sun, caught the eye of his older brother Levi. "Oh brother! Here comes that dreamer Joseph"

"Now is our chance!" one of the brothers said.

"Let's get rid of Joseph and his dreams once and for all! Let's kill him and throw his body into this pit here in the wilderness. We can say a wild animal ate him. There is no one around. Father is far away. Who will know?"

They thought no one could see them.

But, they were wrong. Someone COULD see them.

GOD could see them.

"Great plan!" one brother said to the other.

"Good idea!"

"Let's do it!"

But something inside the heart of the oldest brother Reuben told him that he should be looking out for his little brother - not looking to kill him. And so he said, "No, let's just throw him into the pit - we don't want his blood on our hands." Secretly, he was planning to come back later and rescue his little brother.

So when Joseph got near enough, they grabbed him.

They ripped off his fancy coat - the one they were so jealous of - and threw Joseph into a hole in the ground.

These were his very own brothers, the ones he looked up to, the ones he loved so much.

Joseph looked up from the pit with tears in his eyes.

He felt so alone. His brothers hated him, his father was far away.

But he wasn't alone. God was with him, even in that deep, dark pit.

Meanwhile, it was getting late in the morning, and the brothers were hungry. "Hey, isn't it time for lunch?" Dan said.

They cared more about their own stomachs than they cared about their brother. And that's what causes most of the trouble in the world.

And so they sat down for lunch.

"Pass me Reuben's sandwich!" Dan said.

Just then, a caravan of Ishmaelites came riding by.

The Ishmaelites' camels were loaded with things to sell in Egypt. And that gave Judah an idea.

"Hey, guys!" Judah said. "Let's be traders too! We can sell Joseph to these Ishmaelites. That way we can get rid of Joseph and make some money on the deal besides!"

And so, that's just what they did.

They pulled poor, dirty and bewildered Joseph from the pit and sold him to the Ishmaelites for 20 pieces of silver. That's all their little brother was worth to them.

Now, you might think it was just lucky for Joseph that that caravan came by when it did. But it wasn't luck at all. That caravan could have come by yesterday, or it could have come by tomorrow. But, no, God sent that caravan at just the right time - just like he always does.

God is always at work. And God has a plan.

www.ingramcontent.com/pod-product-compliance
Lightning Source LLC
LaVergne TN
LVHW060509170826
845677LV00026B/1671
* 9 7 9 8 8 6 9 4 5 8 3 2 2 *